Being Resilient

David Tuffley

To my beloved Nation of Four
Concordia Domi – Foris Pax

"The greatest weapon against stress is the ability to choose one thought over another."
— *William James*

Altiora

Published 2014 by Altiora Publications
AltioraPublications.com/

ISBN-13: 978-1505429800   ISBN-10: 1505429803

About the Author

David Tuffley PhD is a Lecturer in Applied Ethics & Socio-Technical Studies at Griffith University in Australia. David has written widely on Applied Psychology topics.

Facebook: www.facebook.com/tuffley/

Acknowledgements

I acknowledge the work of Abraham Maslow, Martin Seligman, Danah Zohar and Howard Gardner.

Also the *Turrbal* and *Jagera* indigenous peoples, on whose ancestral land I write this book.

Contents

Introduction

Resilience, or the ability to handle stress in a positive way, it is an essential ability in your repertoire of life skills. With it, you can meet the challenges of life, grow as a person and approach your full potential as a human being. Without resilience, you become bogged in the problems that you encounter along the road and find it difficult to get yourself out and continue your journey.

Resilience is a form of learned optimism, a process by which you learn to accept that in life, problems will come your way, many of which you have little or no control over. But here is the crucial point, you also realize that you do have control over how you think about and react to those problems. As Shakespeare observed there is *nothing either good or bad that thinking makes it so*. The world you live in is not fixed; it is created by *you*, by your perceptions of what happens around you and how you choose to think about them.

Resilience is a learnable skill; it can be cultivated even if you are not a naturally resilient person. This concise book outlines how you can develop your own resilience and find ways to greater enjoyment and fulfilment in life.

Chapter 1: Building Resilience

Building resilience is a process that you can begin right now, and if you commit to performing this process and developing the mind-set factors outlined in this book, you *will* become a more resilient person, someone able to respond positively when adversity comes your way. These are proven factors that have been the subject of clinical studies over time. They work for others, and there is no reason why they will not work for you.

Optimism

Resilience is fundamentally about being optimistic, about choosing to view events through the lens of optimism rather than pessimism. This is an outlook that can definitely be cultivated, as evidenced by the many positive thinking self-help books on the market.

Basically, cultivate the self-awareness that allows you to notice when you are thinking pessimistically and consciously replace the negative thought with a positive one. It is a conscious process of choosing to think positively.

This is not to suggest that you become blind to the dangers that might exist in a situation. These should be taken careful note of, but they should not be given more weight than they deserve. As a realistic optimist, you go into situations with your eyes wide open and a positive frame of mind.

View Difficulties as Challenges

When problems occur, and it is inevitable that they will, the resilient person sees them as challenges that can be learned from, even when the experience is unpleasant. You cultivate the willingness to be taken out of your comfort zone long enough for a valuable lesson to be learned. And it *is* valuable. It may seem to be just another bothersome complication in your life, but hidden in there is a valuable lesson. So look for the value and take it on board.

If you have ever wondered why the same problems keep coming your way, it is usually because you are not recognising what the experience is trying to teach you. So it keeps happening until you do finally learn the lesson.

Keep in mind the old saying that *life does not always give you what you want, but it will always give you what you need* for your growth as a human being.

A common challenge is how you react when you do not succeed at something. Instead of taking it as a sign from the Universe and give up, you bounce back and look for what you might do differently, then try again with an attitude of *I'm going to keep trying until I find the way that does work*, knowing that it will be tremendously satisfying when that time arrives.

Commitment to Purpose

Develop a strong sense of purpose in life; your reason to get out of bed and be an active agent in the world. Furthermore, you are strongly committed to achieving your purpose and stubbornly refuse to let anything stop you for long.

The reward you get for your efforts comes primarily from the inner satisfaction of knowing you are living a life of significance. Any honours or recognition you receive for your efforts are of secondary importance.

This sense of purpose is like a compass needle that is a constant reminder of the direction you need to be travelling. It can be especially useful when one is confronted by distractions and confusion that would otherwise knock you off course.

Focus on What *Can* be Controlled

Going back to Roman times with the Stoic school of philosophy, the wise person disciplines their thinking to only concerns themselves with what lies *within their control*. They steadfastly refuse to worry about what lies beyond their control. This one, simple, practical idea can save you from wasting an enormous amount of time and effort, thus allowing you to channel your energies into those activities that *will* bring results.

Doing this overtime will help you to feel confident and empowered, while your neighbour who worries needlessly feels powerless and resentful.

This Too Shall Pass

Optimistically remind yourself that there will *always* be an end to what is happening now. Every situation, both good and bad will finish sooner or later, and this will often signal the arrival of the opposite condition.

In time you may become tired of the incessant back and forth pendulum swing of good times and bad. In the interests of a more peaceful life, you may decide to cultivate the habit of reacting situations in ways that do not cause reactions, or least to keep them to a minimum; the so-called middle path in life.

Inner peace lies within your power to achieve, but the price may be too high; giving up one's dependence on the drama. You cannot have good times without the bad, they are two sides of the same coin.

Compartmentalize

As a resilient person, you understand that a set-back in one area of your life does not apply to unrelated areas. You are able to compartmentalise the various parts of your life and keep them separate for their own good.

Keeping things compartmentalized means that a problem in one area does not come to pervade the rest of your life, a situation that can lead to depression and low self-esteem and a host of other problems.

So you may have been unsuccessful at getting that job or that promotion, but it does not mean that you are bad parent or partner in your personal life. Your girlfriend or boyfriend has just told you that it is time to move on in separate directions, but this doesn't mean you can never have a successful relationship – just not with this person.

Personalization

When bad things happen, you do not take it personally by blaming yourself wholly and solely. Events always have multiple causes; you may have contributed to the outcome, but so have others. Instead of beating yourself up, you learn from it and resolve to act differently when a similar situation occurs in the future.

This is a rational approach to understanding the web of cause and effect that operates all around us in the world. You learn that there is a link between what you did in the past and what is happening now. Once you understand how that link works, you can apply it in the present moment to cause the outcomes you want in the future.

Support Network

Everyone needs someone. Even if you are the kind of person who prides themselves on being independent, there will be times when you need the support of other people. In reality, all we really need is a few really good, close friends, people we can turn to for help and support when needed. In many cases you can count these true friends on the fingers of one hand.

True friends are hard to come by and are worth their weight in gold. The rest of those who you would also call friend will be *situational* in nature; you work with them or otherwise find yourselves in each other's company and find you get along. That's OK as long as you can tell the difference between the true friend and situational friend. True friends will always find a way to connect, even across great distances. Situational friends drop away when you change jobs or move house or circumstances otherwise change.

In the dislocated world of today where people find themselves living and working in places where they have no support network, the counselling profession has grown to meet the demand. Spiritual advisors, including priests, rabbis and imams can be of great help for followers of a particular faith. All religions contain helpful advice for people encountering the inevitable problems of life.

For Every Problem There is a Solution

As difficult as some problems might seem, there is *always* a solution. The problem and the solution are two sides of the same coin. One cannot exist without the other. This is not to say that the solution will necessarily be easy. It might be difficult and require some courage and determination to implement, but it is a solution nonetheless.

As someone with resilience, you remind yourself that how you perceive and react to a situation is entirely at your discretion. As Stephen Covey observed, *in the space between what happens to you and what you do about it lies your power to choose.* He was remarking upon Victor Frankl's realisation as he was being tortured in a Nazi concentration camp that no matter what they did to him, he retained the power to decide how he would think about it. He refused to surrender to victimhood. His resilience would have been a key factor in surviving the Holocaust.

Instead of despairing, giving up and otherwise surrendering to an apparently bad situation, you insist on taking the view that even this situation has a solution and that you will find it and implement it whatever it takes.

Change is Inevitable

It is one of the great truisms of life that everything changes, and yet it is so easy to become invested in the *status quo* and not want things to change. Deep down we probably know our life will change sooner or later, but it is easy to lose sight of this reality and become overly attached to the way things are. Eventually, life will simply wrench the status quo from your grip and that will be distressing. Accepting that change is ultimately good will help you lessen the stress of having something taken from you by force.

The resilient person moves with the times, embraces change and tries to be proactive. That way you are at the forefront of change, not lagging behind, being dragged kicking into the future. You do not want to be someone who thinks their best days are behind them and nostalgically clings to their glory days. Your best days lie ahead.

In the end, some of your goals may become superseded by changing circumstances, making the wise move to simply go with the flow. But if the goal remains within your power to achieve, then pursue it with all your energy.

Goal-Oriented

Being goal-oriented keeps you moving, gives you the momentum to make progress in life. Without goals, your rate of progress slows down. The important point about setting goals is that they should be realistic, and be made up of a series of achievable sub-goals that give you reinforcing encouragement. Neither too hard nor too easy, you build your resilience by working through them, solving problems as you go and getting stronger and more confident with every success.

Goals can be seen as a kind of self-fulfilling prophecy that you yourself create. Once you have a worthy goal that can be broken down into achievable stages, and that you are investing daily with the energy of thought and feeling, you automatically begin to move towards it. In an ideal world, if nothing intervenes to knock you off your trajectory towards the goal, you will eventually reach it.

But of course, life usually inserts a few tricky, apparently random events to complicate matters. As a resilient person, you take corrective action to get yourself back on track to achieving your goal(s). You do not let these goal-frustrating events stop you, realizing that each one has given you a valuable lesson to add to your storehouse of know-how and making you are more capable person.

Being goal-oriented helps you be resilient because the things that happen in your daily life become a means to an end. They are not the end itself, so you will be more likely to simply roll over the top of difficulties and not let them stop you.

Decisive

When difficulties arise, the resilient person remains calm, thinks clearly and logically about the situation and forms a plan of action. An essential part of this process is the willingness to actually face the situation and decide to do something.

Many people will try to avoid facing the problem, hoping that it will simply go away. This avoidance creates a sense of victimhood that is not at all helpful.

The fear of making the wrong decision is a major factor in people's unwillingness to be decisive. They might also be afraid of looking foolish for having made the wrong choice. Remember that even if you make a decision that does not immediately lead to a solution, it was still worth making it, since it has brought you one step closer to the solution, if not the solution itself.

Remind yourself that while you are outside of your comfort zone, it is OK since it is all part of a larger process of living and growing as a person. It will be over in due course and you will be back in your comfort zone soon enough.

Grow as a Person

Suffering hardship and loss is no fun at the time, but it can also be the catalyst for rapid growth as a person if viewed through the lens of optimism. It becomes apparent later, with the benefit of hindsight. There is nothing like hardship to teach you who you really are under the layers of social conditioning.

Resilient people grow from the experience of adversity, while non-resilient people allow it to defeat them. It has often been observed that some of the most successful people around experienced great hardship earlier in their life, and it were this that made them what they are. Hardship can make or break you – don't let it break you.

Chapter 2: Cognitive Behaviour Therapy (CBT)

CBT is the general name for the kind of therapy that aims to change the way you think and act. It is an effective therapy for helping sufferers of a range of problems, including people who would benefit by overcoming their fears and negative attitudes to become more resilient.

CBT comes in two parts; the *cognitive* component where you examine and restructure the way you are thinking about a situation, and the *behavioural* component – how your actions are contributing to a problem. Action follows thought, so the therapy starts with becoming aware of how you are currently thinking.

The mind is habit-driven. We develop patterns of thinking that become established as habits over time. In the same way that flowing water wears a deeper and wider channel as time goes by, so too do our mental habits make more established neural pathways in our brains. Just as it is possible to alter the course of a stream by redirecting the water, it is also possible to change established thought patterns and their neural pathways.

Changing a habitual way of thinking is not an easy thing to do. With sustained effort though, CBT can systematically change those troublesome thought patterns. It is not quick fix, but it *does* work.

CBT takes a practical, problem-solving approach in which specific trigger points are identified. Once you know what these points are, you shine the light of logic and reason upon them. You keep the spotlight on the problem until you are able to re-frame the thought in a more constructive way. This is how you unlearn your existing habits and replace them with new ones that are easier to live with.

Mindfulness

Present moment focus (otherwise known as mindfulness) is a key element of CBT. There is nothing mysterious about mindfulness; it is simply a state of *heightened present moment awareness* where you monitor the thought-patterns running through your mind. Aside from CBT, mindfulness is an essential skill for personal growth. In terms of CBT though, you are looking for the thoughts that trigger a negative mood, for example feeling powerless and demotivated in the face of problems.

By focussing on your thoughts in the present moment, you are able to snap out of the tendency to worry about the past and the future where you are powerless to do anything. Your attention is on the here and now, which is the only real time and place that you have in life.

Restructuring your thought patterns

In CBT, the key is to raise your awareness of the thoughts that are causing you problems, in this case preventing you from becoming more resilient. You then challenge them like you would an overbearing associate who is used to bossing you about. Then you can actively replace those troublesome thoughts with something more positive and realistic.

The process outlined here can be applied to help with any of the factors that lead to a more resilient frame of mind. For example, you can use it to:

- replace pessimism with optimism,
- cultivate a sense of purpose over a sense of aimless futility,
- cultivate a focus on what you *can* control rather than what is beyond your control,
- know that a problem is temporary, not permanent,
- know that every problem does in fact have a solution and is not hopeless,
- know that change is inevitable and must be embraced rather than sticking nostalgically to the past,

- know that being decisive is better than leaving a problem to fix itself, and also
- that becoming goal-oriented is better than simply hoping for the best.

Try doing this:

Become aware of your negative thoughts. These are usually what are going through your mind just before you start thinking pessimistically. Unless you make the conscious effort to identify these thoughts they will probably pass through and be gone without you even being aware of them. Once the pessimism sets in, thoughts are replaced by the feelings that were triggered by the thought.

Pessimists usually perceive situations as being worse than they actually are. A thought is catastrophized and taken to its limit.

Challenge your negative thoughts. This second step is about using *logic* to refute the pessimistic thought that you identified in the previous step. Rationality has to triumph over irrationality.

Taking a deep breath and repeating a calming mantra to help you relax, you question what evidence there might be for the pessimistic thought to be true.

Exchange the negative for the positive. Having gone through the rational process of testing the truth of those negative thoughts and found them to be false or at least exaggerated, you then deliberately replace them with positive, rational thoughts.

Chapter 3:
Exposure Therapy

Used in conjunction with CBT or by itself, exposure therapy helps you to master the negative attitudes that keep you from becoming more resilient. You do this by exposing yourself to a graded set of fear-inducing situations, beginning with very mild, and progressing to the next, slightly more fearful situation, mastering that and so on all the way up to the ultimate terror.

As difficult as it might seem, often the simple act of making the decision to not run from your fears any more, to turn and face them and refuse to be bullied by them any more, can be a powerfully transformative moment. It is an act of courage that can pay big dividends. 'Avoidance', as Psychologists call it, can keep you down and feeling powerless to take constructive action. The longer it goes on, the worse the situation becomes.

If you can find the courage to face your fears, to deliberately and defiantly take yourself out of your comfort zone by placing yourself in the very situation(s) that make you uneasy, and if you can use the thought-restructuring techniques and breathing/relaxation techniques to stay cool calm and collected, then you will have made a giant step towards controlling your fear instead of the fear controlling you.

For example, if leaving your comfort zone upsets you and all you can think about is getting back there, make the conscious choice to *allow* yourself to be uncomfortable for as long as it takes to resolve the situation. Step outside of yourself and look back with objectivity at the you who is in that situation and feeling uncomfortable. Use that detachment to build your tolerance to the discomfort.

Remind yourself that outside of your comfort zone is the only place you can grow as a human being and that a period of discomfort is worth it for the benefits and satisfaction of having grown as a person.

Progressively facing your fears

Starting with a very small challenge to your ability to be resilient and progressing up, over time, to greater and more difficult challenges is an excellent method for anyone who wanting to overcome their seeming inability to do any number of things.

You can start by making a list of situations that are likely to cause you to give up, get depressed, take it personally etc. (see list in previous chapter). Order the list from the mildest challenge through 15 or more stages to the scariest, most stressful scenario. This has been called a 'hierarchy of fear' and it works by progressively desensitizing you to stressful situations and lessening your anxiety.

The key to this technique is to manage your expectations as to how fast it will work. It takes time, and it is necessary to be patient. Each step must be taken by concentrating on reducing your anxiety using the breathing and relaxation techniques.

Approach the nerve-wracking business of facing your fears in the full knowledge that it is within your abilities to overcome the debilitating fears that have been controlling your life.

For example, if meeting strangers makes you anxious, you could start going to a party with an extraverted friend. Practice the rational thinking and breathing relaxation to become comfortable with this challenge, repeating until you have become comfortable with it. Then you can progress to introducing yourself to a stranger and so on.

Remember, patience and persistence is the key to success with this technique. The process will take as long as it takes, and that is OK. After all, you are re-routing the neural pathways I your brain and that is not a quick process.

Relax & Breath

At the heart of most relaxation techniques is a simple three stage process. First, with full conscious awareness take ten deep breaths, in through the nose, out through the mouth, using the diaphragm and not your ribcage to fill your lungs. Don't be in a hurry to finish, savour every breath and take simple pleasure in the fact that you are alive and there is air to breath. Second, on the out-breath silently say to yourself *'I am relaxed'* – don't just say it though, you have to *feel it.* Third, when you have finished your breaths, actively see yourself fearlessly doing the thing that you previously felt afraid of. Make this image as vivid in your imagination as you can, turn it into a movie if that helps. Just see it happening and believe that if you can imagine it in your inside world, you can perform in the outside world.

This is a powerful technique that is used by high performing, successful individuals in all walks of life from Prime Ministers and Presidents to Navy SEALs.

Make Your List

List out 10 to 20 situations that make you feel demotivated, depressed, lacking in confidence etc. Order them from mild to severe.

If your goal is to bounce back after a relationship breakdown, loss of job or rejection by peers, begin by seeing yourself doing just that; bouncing back. You make a movie in your mind and see yourself shrugging off the set-back and continuing on with your life, stronger and more confident than you were before. Tell yourself this is the real you, the person you are becoming. This is how you create a new, resilient mind-set.

Work Through the List

Using the relaxation technique outlined in the first step above, work your way through the list from easy to hard. Stay in each situation for as long as it takes to feel the negative emotion subside. You will need to repeat the relaxation technique every day, several times a day, investing the positive movie-in-your-mind with positive emotion and the expectation that this is who you are becoming.

The whole process should be done every day for at least a month. Research shows that this is how long it takes, at a minimum, for significant changes to become real in your life. Do not expect to finish it quickly, and *do* expect to have to repeat each step several times until you feel quite comfortable.

Your Associates

To become more resilient, seek out and associate with resilient people.

It is simple fact of human nature that we become like the people we associate with. The more time we spend in someone's company, the more like them we become and *vice versa*. This tendency is hard-wired into the human species, largely because in our evolutionary past, survival depended on having a support group around us. The world was a dangerous place, and loners were vulnerable to predation.

Chapter 4:
Self-Actualization

Abraham Maslow is well-known for his work on the hierarchy of human needs. Basic needs must be satisfied before you become aware of higher order needs. The hierarchy is represented as a pyramid, with the basic needs at the pyramid's broad base, and with self-actualisation at the apex. A Self-Actualised person has found a way to satisfy all of his or her lower needs and has cultivated the conscious awareness of their highest self. They allow this awareness to express itself more fully in their lives.

Becoming a more resilient person, someone who persists and does not give up when they do not at first succeed, is a pre-requisite for becoming self-actualized.

The achievement of Self-Actualisation is recognised by Maslow as a human need, so in a sense it is everyone's birth right to be self-actualised.

The need for Self-Actualisation asserts itself once we have satisfied the lowest-order needs for food, shelter, sex, then middle-order needs for safety and security, then the higher middle-order needs for love and belonging. Above these is the higher-order need for self-esteem. The highest need of all, sitting like the capstone of a pyramid is the need for Self-Actualisation.

The annals of various religions tell us that a person can achieve the highest expression of their human potential with only some or none of the higher and middle order needs being met, and with only the barest of lower-order needs like food and shelter being satisfied. This is more difficult, requiring you to become an ascetic recluse and engage in mortification of the flesh to free yourself of these normal human needs. The author is *not* recommending this course of action. Our body is not an impediment to self-actualization and happiness. Quite the opposite, it is a great ally. We owe it to ourselves to take the best care of our body that we can by eating well, getting enough exercise and rest, and avoiding toxic and/or addictive substances.

We all have the same set of hierarchical needs but the unique circumstances of our lives means that the way we go about satisfying them will be different for every individual. What follows is not a prescription for achieving self-actualization; rather it is a description of the mind-set of self-actualizing people that anyone can emulate in their own life. It paints a portrait that you can model yourself after.

Experience Things Fully, Vividly, Selflessly

Self-Actualised (SA) people throw themselves wholeheartedly into the experiences that come their way; concentrating on it fully, allowing it to fully absorb them.

The only way this can be done is to be (a) mindful, that is fully conscious in the present moment and (b) fully accepting of the circumstances of that moment. In other words, you are fully aware and accepting of whatever situation you find yourself in.

This is easier said than done because most of the time we impose judgment on situations and in the process we alienate ourselves from it. Soon we are thinking we would like to be somewhere else.

In terms of achieving your full potential, mindfulness is about using an evolved part of your brain that many people do not use. It lays dormant, waiting for the command to awaken.

You can awaken this part of your brain by simply deciding (and following through on the decision) to observe the on-going activity in your own mind. Using a computer metaphor, you activate a monitoring program that watches what is going on.

This phenomenon can be described as metaconsciousness, or thinking about thinking. It is a *new dimension of consciousness* that humans are capable of that no other intelligent species can manage. There is the part of you that thinks your normal thoughts, and then there is the part that observes you thinking those thoughts. Previously there was only the thinker. Now there is the thinker and the observer.

Awakening the observer, this higher dimension of thought, is an important aspect of becoming Self-Actualised.

Mindfulness also helps you to stop thinking so much about the past and the future by removing the dimension of time from your thinking.

In the Now you observe the world of phenomena in a judgment-free way. You accept it without mental resistance, understanding that this resistance is what prevents you from experiencing every moment of your life as the best moment.

On-going Choice Between Safety and Risk

Your life is a moment-by-moment choice between safety (out of fear and need for defence) and risk (for the sake of progress and growth): SA people consciously make the growth choice many times a day.

If you observe your own mind in action (as in previous section) you will notice that this continuum (with safety at one end and risk at the other) is often active in your thinking.

There is a dynamic tension between these two opposites, and you will habitually lean towards one or the other. If you are like many people, you are probably inclined towards the safe, low-risk option because you want predictability and comfort with no unpleasant surprises.

A Self-Actualising person may still value comfort and security, but they know that personal growth is slow for as long as they remain in their comfort-zone. They therefore take themselves out of their comfort zone as often as they can in order to create the right conditions for Self-Actualisation.

A life well-lived will always involve both pleasure and pain. Deep acceptance of this fact is essential for personal growth.

Let Your True Self Emerge

SA people try to go beyond socially-defined modes of thinking and feeling. They let their inner experience tell them what they truly feel.

When in doubt, be honest. It may take some courage, but SA people look honestly at themselves and take responsibility for who they are and what happens to them. Self-delusion is the enemy of self-actualisation.

If you are monitoring your thinking and behaviour, you might notice that much of what you think and do conforms to what you believe people expect of you.

To the greatest extent possible, you should listen to what your intuition is telling you about people and situations and behave according to this more reliable guide. As you become Self-Actualised, the voice of your intuition becomes stronger because you are listening to it more. You recognise it as a reliable, in-built guidance mechanism that always has your best interests foremost.

There are times when we need to conform to certain behavioural standards in order to get along in the world. The challenge is finding a way of harmonising or reconciling what your intuition is telling you and how the world expects you to behave when the two are at variance.

The idea is expressed perfectly in Shakespeare's Hamlet, where Polonius gives this most valuable advice to his son; *This above all: to thine own self be true, And it must follow, as the night the day, Thou canst not then be false to any man.*

Listen To Your Own Tastes

SA people are prepared to be unpopular if necessary.

The SA person does not look for trouble, but when there is a conflict between what they inwardly know is right, and what everyone else is saying, a SA person has the courage to disagree with the group and risk their disapproval or ostracism.

When we receive disapproval, it is profoundly uncomfortable. Most of us will do anything to avoid it. That usually means compliantly going along in order to get along. Disapproval is an instrument of control that opinion-leaders use to enforce conformist behaviour. Membership of a group is contingent on conforming to group norms.

Approval is the other side of the same coin; behaviour that conforms to group expectations is rewarded and reinforced. Approval and disapproval together form the standard "carrot and stick" approach to motivating people.

Group-think and blind conformity is anathema to the SA person.

The SA person recognises when the people around them use approval and/or disapproval to try to influence their behaviour. Their challenge is finding a way to maintain their integrity without creating unnecessary conflict.

Use Your Intelligence

SA people work to do well the things they do, no matter how insignificant those things seem. They understand that greatness comes not so much from what you do, but how well you do the things you do no matter how big or small they are.

SA people know that great satisfaction comes from focussing fully on the task in front of them, and doing that task to the absolute best of their ability.

There is tremendous satisfaction in doing everything as well as you can, even the small, seemingly unimportant things. Doing this keeps your mind firmly in the present moment, the only time and place where you can truly be alive.

The task itself is not as important as the creation in yourself of an attitude of excellence, which is another way of saying living to your fullest potential.

You no longer think that near enough is good enough, that economy of effort and taking it easy as much as you can is the best way to live. These are self-limiting attitudes that will keep you in the realm of mediocrity.

When you live this way, *every moment becomes the best moment of your life.*

Make Peak Experiencing More Likely

Get rid of illusions and false notions. SA people find out what it is they are good at, and what they are not good at.

Being honest with yourself about this is a foundation for Self-Actualisation. SA people are honest, even brutally honest with themselves at every level of their lives. What they aim for is congruency between their inner and outer worlds.

Honesty will eventually create harmony inside and outside of being. Nature cannot lie to itself, but humans do lie to themselves and in so doing create a false inner world. By ridding yourself of delusion, your inner world comes into alignment with the outer world, creating harmony.

So, honesty creates the right conditions to have deep insight into the nature of the world you live in. This is the insight that leads you to Self-Actualisation.

Know Thyself

SA people ask themselves who are you, what are you, what is good and what is bad for you, where you are going, what is your mission?

Opening yourself up like this allows you to recognize your defences that stand in the way of ultimate fulfilment. The challenge then is to find the courage to let them go.

Coming to deep self-knowledge is a life-time endeavour. In ancient times, it was believed that only by knowing your inner world, the microcosm, can you come to have knowledge of the outer world, the macrocosm. The micro is a miniature of the macro, correct in every detail in the way that a fragment of a hologram contains full detail of the whole.

Characteristics of Self-Actualised People

This section outlines the characteristics shared by self-actualizing people everywhere, regardless of culture.

Realistically oriented with an efficient perception of reality extending into all areas of life. SA people are unthreatened by the unknown. They have a superior ability to think clearly and logically, allowing them to arrive at an understanding of the truth of a situation.

Accept oneself, others and the natural world the way they are. SA people see human nature as it really is, not as the people around them think it ought to be. Furthermore they have rid themselves of crippling guilt; they act with integrity in the way they know is right and are therefore able to enjoy themselves without regret or apology. They have no unnecessary inhibitions.

Spontaneous in their inner life, thoughts and impulses. SA people are unhampered by convention. Their ethics are autonomous, they see themselves as an individual, and are motivated towards continual improvement.

Focus on problems outside oneself. SA people have a mission in life that requires much energy; their mission is their reason to live. Sure of its rightness, they are usually serene and worry-free as they pursue their mission with unstoppable determination.

Detachment, the need for privacy. Alone but not lonely, SA people retain their composure amid confusion and personal misfortunes. They are like the hero of Rudyard Kipling's poem If … *if you can keep your head when all about you are losing theirs and blaming it on you*. SA people are self-starters, responsible for themselves. They own their behaviour.

Autonomous, independent of culture and environment. SA people rely on their inner self for satisfaction. Resilient and stable in the face of hard knocks, SA people are self-contained, independent from the love and respect of others in the sense that they can resist attempts to use these to manipulate them.

Freshness of appreciation. SA people have a fresh rather than stereotyped appreciation of people and things. Moment to moment living is thrilling, transcendent and spiritual. SA people live the present moment to the fullest.

Peak experiences. In Maslow's words *"Feelings of limitless horizons opening up to the vision, the feeling of being simultaneously more powerful and also more helpless than one ever was before, the feeling of ecstasy and wonder and awe, the loss of placement in time and space with, finally, the conviction that something extremely important and valuable had happened, so that the subject was to some extent transformed and strengthened even in his daily life by* *such experiences. When peak experiences are especially powerful, the sense of self dissolves into an awareness of a greater unity."* (from Religion, Values and Peak Experiences, 1970).

The way Maslow describes Self-Actualised people is very similar to the way a person who has achieved Satori in Zen is described. They are qualitatively the same experience. This is a natural human state, albeit a one that few people have yet reached, but one which is achievable with commitment and effort.

Chapter 5:
Lifestyle

Being resilient is greatly helped by cultivating good habits, and practicing them daily.

Have an Annual Health Check

Understand that your health is *your* responsibility, not your doctor's. Take charge of your health by scheduling an annual wellness check-up with your doctor to actively maintain good health. Do not wait until you get sick to visit the doctor.

Proactively avoid becoming sick by having the doctor give you a thorough check-up to identify potential problems before they become an *actual* problem. For example, your blood pressure or cholesterol may be too high, you may be heading towards diabetes, your prostate might be enlarged, there might be polyps growing in your large intestine, there may be a lump in your breast. All of these can be fatal if left too long. Treated in time, the problem is eliminated easily.

Examine the cause of death of your parents, uncles and aunts, your grandparents and their siblings on both sides of the family. This will give you a good indication of what your most likely problems are going to be.

Walk at Least 30 Minutes a Day

Walking is the perfect exercise. Our bodies have evolved to walk long distances; though a sedentary lifestyle may make the idea of walking several kilometres a day seem much too strenuous.

Walking is classed as aerobic exercise. This improves the efficiency of your lungs to absorb oxygen, and your heart's ability to pump that oxygen to all parts of your body. Walking does not just exercise your legs. Your upper body is also participating; you swing your arms and rotate your trunk as you go.

Walking is also an opportunity to notice the myriad things, large and small, that exist unnoticed in your environment. It is worth it because there is extraordinary beauty just waiting to be experienced. Don't just walk with tunnel vision; look about you, hear the sounds, smell the smells, notice the complex patterns of Nature. Look for the beauty that is all around. As the old saying goes, *what you seek is also seeking you*. Do you want beautiful things to manifest in your life? Seek them out, and they will find you.

Take your time, be in the moment, cultivate a sense of gratitude that you are alive and able to walk around. You will be richly rewarded if you do this.

This kind of mindful walking can be the foundation of your daily exercise regime. Around 30 minutes a day or more gives you the required amount of aerobic exercise while nourishing your mind and spirit.

Sense of Humour

Laughter is a universal human phenomenon. Everyone, everywhere instinctively does it, and understands why others do it, regardless of language or culture. Science does not have a good understanding of why we laugh, but it has been recognised that it is a key element in social bonding. We like people who make us laugh. Incidentally, it is thought that the origins of laughter are in releasing the tension and expressing the shared relief at the passing of danger.

The ability to see the humorous side of life is about resiliency. Humour has a curiously life-enhancing effect because it requires an optimistic mind-set.

Laughter is a natural way for you to experience free and simple enjoyment of life. Research shows that it directly creates a range of healthy physical changes in the body. It strengthens the immune system, releases endorphins that promotes feelings of well-being and reduces pain, improves blood circulation, boosts energy, reduces conflict between people and overall works to lessen the damaging effects of stress.

A good belly-laugh relaxes your whole body, making it an effective remedy for stress. It has a strengthening effect on the immune system by decreasing the stress hormones that may be present. When these stress hormones are present, the immune system has a more difficult task in fighting infection.

Laughter releases endorphins -- these are naturally released under a variety of circumstances including exercise, excitement (for example laughter), pain, consumption of spicy food, love and sexual excitement. Endorphins produce an analgesic effect and a feeling of well-being.

Laughter protects the heart. Laughter improves the function of blood vessels and increases blood flow, which can help protect you against a heart attack and other cardiovascular problems. Try to adopt a mind-set that can appreciate the funny side of life.

Maintain an Active Lifestyle

The best kind of exercise is natural movement that is an integral part of your normal lifestyle. Going to the gymnasium, performing a daily exercise regime might be enjoyable for highly disciplined people, but the majority of us will struggle to maintain any exercise regime over years and decades. It seems too much like hard work.

Exercise regimes are unnecessary if your life involves a moderate amount of natural, low-impact movement such as walking, swimming, cycling, gardening or anything else you like. The key is to *enjoy* it. You will want to keep doing what you enjoy.

Avoid high-impact sports that stress bones and joints. Over time, those joints will wear out and become inflamed and painful due to overuse. Remember, people in the evolutionary past rarely lived past middle age, so while they often had to exert themselves greatly, their bodies did not need to last very long by today's standards.

You cannot keep doing the strenuous things you used to do when you were young and expect your body to keep working. Expending upwards of 3,000 to 3,500 calories over the course of the day will give you the right balance.

Studies have shown that inactive people do not live as long as active people, and the group that lives the longest burns about 3,000 to 3,500 calories per day.

Be a Gardener

Related to the previous section, gardening is one of the best possible ways of getting the physical exercise you need while doing something enjoyable.

There is something profoundly satisfying about cultivating plants in your own garden. Beyond the obvious benefits of creating your own super-fresh food, it is profoundly satisfying at an instinctive level to dig in the earth, feel the texture of it in your hands, smell those earthy smells, plant seeds, water them, watch them grow, pull out weeds and so on. Being an unhurried gardener can add years to your life.

Exercise Your Brain

No less important than exercising your body is exercising your brain. Your brain consumes around 30% of your body's energy, far greater than any other organ.

Nearly a third of all of the energy created by the digestion of food goes to generating the electrical impulses of the brain and central nervous system. Simply put, your brain is an expensive organ to run, so it is not surprising that people have a tendency to use it less. But to stay young and live long, it is vitally important that the brain be kept fully functional and not allowed to wither away through not enough use.

Find something new and interesting to occupy your mind with every day. It does not matter too much what it is, though it helps if you consider it to be meaningful and contributing to your purpose in life.

Keep learning; learn a new language, a musical instrument, take up a hobby, do crosswords and jigsaw puzzles. Do any or all of these things and more to keep your brain young.

Build Strong Bones

Strong bones can be built through daily activity that exerts weight on the bones. As with every other part of your body, if you do not use it, you lose it. Astronauts who spend extended periods of weightlessness are known to suffer from a marked decrease in bone density because their bodies no longer need the bone density needed on Earth.

Sitting in an armchair or lying on a couch all day is telling your body that it does not need strong bones, so your bone density adjusts to what it needs to be for a sedentary lifestyle.

Keep Your Expectations Low

It has been wisely said that the secret of a long and happy life is to keep your expectations low. You are rarely disappointed and so will avoid getting angry. Often, you will be pleasantly surprised when your low expectations are exceeded.

Look around you in the world. The people who complain the most, who express their unhappiness with life are those whose expectations have not been met. Perhaps they were too high in the first place, or perhaps they really did get a raw deal. Either way, being angry and inflicting negativity helps no-one. If there really has been an injustice, it can be settled amicably. There is no need to become a door-mat when maintaining low expectations.

Get Some Sun, But Not Too Much

The sun is the source of almost all life on Earth. We definitely need it in our life if we are not to suffer from Vitamin D deficiency which leads to Rickets.

Depending on how much melanin pigmentation you have in your skin, for good health you need to get some exposure to the sun, preferably every day. Too much sun is a leading cause of skin cancer. In the Australian state of Queensland (where I live) the sun is strong and many people have Scottish ancestry with its red hair and pale skin. Consequently, Queensland has one of the highest rates of skin cancer anywhere in the world, much higher than in Scotland. For people with fair skin, no more than a few minutes a day of direct exposure to the sun without protection is likely to cause problems in the long-term. People with brown or dark brown skin can tolerate more sun.

Massage

Massage, or more precisely therapeutic massage is both relaxing and healing. There is something fundamental in human nature that responds positively to touch. Children who receive too little nurturing touch may survive physically, but their emotional development will have been seriously impaired.

Unfortunately the term 'massage' has become synonymous with various forms of sexual activity. While I do not dismiss the beneficial effects of sexual release for those who need it, the kind of massage being discussed here is of the Swedish, Thai, shiatsu, acupressure kind. These work on a whole of body level to improve the circulation of blood and lymph, release of muscular tension and promote a general sense of well-being.

Listen to Calming Music

Soothing, gentle music is therapeutic because it lessens tension. At a cognitive level, it helps with memory, concentration and reasoning skills. At a physical level, it lowers your blood pressure, elevates your mood, relaxes your muscles and boosts your immune system.

All in all, there is no down-side to listening to calming music. The same cannot be said for highly stimulating music that is fast and frantic. Music is essentially an emotional statement. Your inner world will resonate to the mood of the music being listened to.

Be Flexible in Your Thinking

Related to the previous point, being flexible, like a child is flexible, is an essential aspect of healthy aging. When life serves up a situation that is not what you expect or are accustomed to, do not become cranky and negative. If you cannot change the situation, have the grace to simply accept it with good humour.

Rid Yourself of Addiction

Easier said than done, yet smoking, excessive alcohol consumption or over-consumption of a wide-range of illicit and prescription drugs has a strongly adverse effect on your mental and physical health.

Appendix C of this book gives you a series of nine strategies for beating addiction. For more detailed information see David Tuffley's book *Beating Addiction*.

Ease into The Day

Upon waking in the morning, try not to launch too quickly or energetically into the day. The strain of going from a dormant state to heightened activity can heavily tax your organs, particularly the heart.

The majority of heart attacks and strokes occur in the morning. Go to bed early enough so that you can get up early enough the next morning to give yourself time to ease into the day, rather than sleep in as late as possible, then have to frantically launch into your morning's activities.

The Flame that Burns Twice as Bright

The flame that burns twice as bright burns half as long, as the saying goes. Try to pace yourself to a steady, even pace and avoid extremes if you possibly can. This includes matching your diet with your lifestyle.

If you are relatively inactive, eat a light, preferably vegetarian diet. If you are physically active, a higher protein diet is needed. Eating a high protein, high calorie diet with a sedentary lifestyle will cause weight-gain.

Snoring and Sleep Apnoea

Sleep apnoea is condition where a person stops breathing for a short period while asleep, following by a loud snort as the person gasps for breath. This event can be repeated between 5 and 30 times per hour.

Snoring and sleep apnoea obviously disrupt your breathing while you are unconscious. To starve your body of oxygen while sleeping is obviously not a good thing. It raises your blood pressure and also raises the level of cholesterol in the blood too, leading to a heightened risk of heart attack and stroke. People who die in their sleep often do so as a result of these. Seek medical advice if you suffer from either of these.

Take a Siesta

Studies show that a short nap of about 45 minutes or less (one sleep cycle) in the middle of the day has a highly beneficial effect on a person's health.

Latin cultures have no difficulty accepting the wisdom of this practice. Anglo cultures on the other hand tend to regard a midday snooze as a sign of laziness; hence Noel Coward's whimsical song *mad dogs and Englishmen go out in the midday sun.*

Lose weight and do your heart a favour

It is not difficult to see how carrying around an additional 20 or 30 kilograms can place great strain on your heart. Imagine permanently carrying a back-pack weighing that much. It would be ridiculous and intolerable to place such a handicap on you, yet this is exactly what many people are doing in our obesity-afflicted Western world.

In the course of evolution, humans developed the ability to store body fat because famine was a very real danger. Today, in the absence of some catastrophic event that disrupts society, we are always going to be able to find enough to eat.

Losing weight is easier said than done. Our eating habits become very deeply embedded and are highly resistant to change. Your doctor can advise the best course of action for your situation.

Pace Yourself

When you have a job that requires much physical and/or mental effort, do not try to do it all in one session. You might wish to get it done and out of the way, but the excessive effort will put your body under stress.

Adjust your expectations about how soon the job needs to be finished. Allow it to be open-ended. Then approach the job in manageable chunks. Work for an hour, then rest, work another hour, rest again. Pacing yourself in this way is being kind to your body and avoids over-straining.

Avoid Eating to Ease Emotional Pain

It is well-known that comfort foods like chocolate and other high fat, high sugar and high salt foods can give temporary relief for emotional upset, but at what cost to your health?

Often the habit is established and reinforced in childhood when you were given treats to cheer you up when you were upset, often by somebody that you trusted uncritically.

When done to excess, this is a form of binge eating and really should be brought under control as it will lead to obesity and diabetes. If you address the underlying issue, the food addiction will become manageable. See Appendix C for advice on overcoming addiction.

Aromatherapy

Our sense of smell is tied to a very primitive part of our brain, the so-called 'lizard brain'. The lizard brain operates mostly below the level of conscious thought. It makes its presence felt as powerful emotion.

Smells can therefore exert a powerful influence on our mood. Use this knowledge to your advantage by arranging your living space to have aromas that make you feel calm and relaxed.

There are many helpful books on aromatherapy that you can easily access. In summary though, jasmine helps with depression, lavender with sleeplessness, citrus for mental alertness, peppermint and ginger for poor digestion, eucalyptus for sinus problems. Avoid pungent, unpleasant smells if possible.

Remain Sexually Active

Healthy sexual activity has been compared to the fountain of youth. Sexual intimacy makes us feel connected with and loved by another person. Sex releases a potent cocktail of natural, feel-good substances into the bloodstream (endorphins, DHEA and growth hormone) that promote health and a sense of well-being. These counteract the stress hormones adrenalin and cortisol which may be present as a result of life's trials and tribulations.

There are three basic guidelines that will ensure a positive experience; both parties must be willing participants, be intuitive and spontaneous about what you do and how you do it, and make sure you are meeting your partner's needs as well as your own.

Nurture Loving Family Relationships

Being on close, loving terms with your family has been shown by studies to lengthen a person's life and to improve the quality of that life by creating a strong sense of community, belonging and mutual support.

Be a Good Neighbour

Neighbours are members of your extended family in the sense that what affects you, also affects them. Try to build a relationship of mutual respect and support if necessary. Good neighbours can greatly add to your quality of life. Ask yourself, 'if I had myself as a neighbour, what would I think of me?' Try to be the neighbour that you yourself would want.

Do Not Hold Grudges

Staying angry and holding grudges against people who have done you harm will only succeed in making you sick in the medium to long term. As the old saying goes, being angry with someone is like drinking poison and expecting the other person to die. As difficult as it might be, you MUST let your grievances go if you are to live a long and happy life. Forgiving does not mean forgetting and allowing the same problem to happen again. You need never allow that problem to happen again. it is essential though that you let the past go. Concentrate on what is happening in the present moment and think as little as possible about the past.

Try to Understand, not Judge

As Stephen Covey pointed out, when a person is busy judging others, they are unable to empathise and understand the others. Judgment and understanding are mutually exclusive mind-sets. Making a judgment is to say 'I know everything I need to know about this situation. My mind is now closed to new information.'

Use empathy often to cultivate understanding and compassion for others in the world. They are not so very different from you. If you were in their situation, you might very well act the same.

Self-Reliance

Long-lived people tend to be fiercely independent. They do not expect others to do for them what they are able to do for themselves. The activity and energy required to take care of their daily chores helps to keep them fit.

One reason long-lived people can still take care of themselves in advanced old age is because they have simplified their lives to the point where there is not overly much to do, just a few simple rituals such as tending the garden, going for a walk, feeding the chickens. Cultivate a simple, modest life without a lot of clutter or reliance on consumer goods.

Chapter 6:
Meditation

Meditation at its simplest is best described as *heightened awareness without the mental chatter.* Meditation basically quietens the mind so that you can calmly observe it.

With our often restless minds in control and constantly demanding entertainment, meditation is difficult (to say the least). The method outlined here is the essence of every method, and is so simple that it only takes a few minutes to learn, though perhaps a lifetime to master.

Breathe Rhythmically

Begin by sitting comfortably and breathe rhythmically. Sit with spine straight but in a way that will not induce sleep. Breathe deeply, from the diaphragm, in through your nose and out through your mouth. If you get horizontal, or too comfortable, sleep will not be far away. Sleep is definitely not meditation. Sleep is unconsciousness, absence of awareness.

Focus Your Awareness

Focus your conscious awareness on the place immediately behind the centre of your forehead, the so-called Third Eye, the place where your highest awareness resides. Imagine your attention is a focused beam of light that illuminates and energises your highest awareness where it lives. Generate a strong desire to bring the highest possible awareness into your everyday consciousness. You know that this place is the centre of your inner world, your most sacred place and the very heart of who you are. You know you have succeeded with this step when you have a strong feeling of being centred.

Expand Your Awareness Outwards

While maintaining this feeling of centeredness, allow your attention to expand outwards in all directions. The focussed beam of light now becomes a broadcasting beacon of light radiating out in all directions.

Expanding your awareness outwards like this should give you a sense of spaciousness, ease and lightness. The centring and expansion can proceed almost simultaneously and should involve no further effort beyond the effort to focus and then radiate your attention in the way described. It is not something you should try to do, or force yourself to do. You allow it to happen. It is a natural state of awareness that existed in our distant ancestors before we developed egoic thinking. This spacious but centred awareness is a natural state of mind that you are allowing to become re-established in yourself, not something new that you have to work to establish.

After centring your awareness and then allowing it to expand outwards, continue to **consciously breathe deeply and rhythmically**. Concentrate your awareness on the in-breath without engaging in any mental commentary. Simply be aware of the breath as it comes in, and be likewise aware as it goes out, all the while remaining centred, aware and thoughtless. This is the essence of meditation.

You can count sub-vocally on the out-breath up to a certain number of breaths, (say 50). Or you can set a timer to remind you when ten minutes has passed. Ten minutes is a good duration to begin with. Do the ten minutes for two weeks or so until it becomes well-established, then gradually increase the duration up to 30 minutes over the weeks that follow.

Your goal should be to meditate in this way for up to 30 minutes, twice a day. It is good to begin your day with a meditation session. Likewise end the day with a session in the evening not long before bed-time.

Conclusion

This book presents information and strategies to help you deal with the challenging events that come your way in life. Losing your job or business, relationship break-up, bereavement, illness or disability, and being the victim of crime are all examples of situations where when resilience should come to the fore.

How would *you* react to events of this seriousness? Would it knock the wind out of you such that you would find it difficult to carry on? Or do you have the resilience to get up again and keep moving forwards?

This book aims to help you be the kind of person who bounces back and carries on, stronger than before. It describes what resilience is and how you can cultivate it in your own life so that you can meet those catastrophic events and go on to become a stronger, happier person.

I wish you the very best on your journey.

The End

About the Author

David Tuffley PhD is a Lecturer in Applied Ethics & Socio-Technical Studies at Griffith University in Australia. David has written widely on Applied Psychology topics.

For other books written in the Applied Psychology and other series, visit David's Amazon Author site. (Google on *david tuffley amazon author*)

Join him on Facebook at **facebook.com/tuffley**